I Like - Book 2
VI

By Viola & Zaida Stefano

The rights of Viola & Zaida Stefano to be identified as the authors of this work have been asserted by them in accordance with the **Copyright Amendment (Moral Rights) Act 2000.**

All rights reserved. Apart from any use as permitted by the authors & under the **Copyright Act 1968**, no part may be reproduced, copied, scanned, stored in a retrieval system, recorded, or shared, by any means or in any form, without prior written permission from the publisher.

A catalogue record of this book is available from the **National Library of Australia.**

ISBN: 978-0-6456272-8-2

Authors: Viola Stefano & Zaida Stefano
Illustrations, cover & internal designs: Zaida Stefano

Illustrations copyright © Zaida Stefano 2022
Design copyright © Zaida Stefano 2022

Disclaimer: The content presented in this book is meant for educational purposes only. The authors & publisher claim no accountability to any entity or person for any liability, damage, or loss caused or assumed to be caused directly or indirectly as a consequence of the application, use, or interpretation of the material in this book.

VeeZee Publications

Copyright © VeeZee Publications Pty Ltd 2022
First published in Australia in 2022
by VeeZee Publications Pty Ltd
veezeepublications.com

Learning made easy with

VeeZee!

- Focus Core words in 'I Like - book 2' and the 'I Like' series
- Secondary Core words in 'I Like - book 2' and the 'I Like' series
- Other secondary Core words in the 'I Like' series but **NOT** in 'I Like - book 2'

Core Vocabulary used throughout **VeeZee Publications**				
I	want	can	stop	**look**
like	**more**	**he**	go	see
here	what	**do**	**the**	**and**
out	where	**we**	**it**	**up**
not	**they**	when	**that**	**down**
she	now	them	is	put
help	off	**you**	yes	on
turn	who	**this**	no	why
done	make	a	**to**	under
come	in	some	which	**there**
open	get	good	same	home

Supporting students with low vision (vision impairment - VI)

Our VI range has been especially developed to give children with low vision the very best opportunity to learn. The illustrations in the VI version of the readers, replicate key elements of the photographs included in the other version of the readers. We have done this so that all students engage with the same content. Yellow framing is used around each illustration to support children with low vision to focus on the illustrations more readily. Each book is carefully designed with deliberate and strategic use of colour, background and contrast for typescript and for illustrations. Placing these colours onto a black background supports children with low vision to see the illustrations more successfully because of the contrast provided. Teachers should provide guidance to their students by talking about the colours, lines and themes of each illustration. Ask questions using Core words; who, what, where, when and why, to reinforce their associations with surrounding words. The illustrations with their vibrant colours included in our VI range have been created to promote student interest, engagement and learning. Please ensure that classroom lighting provides optimal conditions for students to engage with the VI readers. We advise that students without a vision impairment also explore the readers designed for students with low vision. This will support interaction and discussion amongst the students. It is our hope that this will ultimately promote acceptance, understanding, compassion and teamwork, thus cultivating true inclusion.

We hope you have fun discovering what creatures are in our 'I Like' books. Not all of them have been named, so good luck with your research!

Book 2 Key Colours

Why are bees so important?

I like it.

You like it.

We like it.

They like it.

Dad likes it.

Mum likes it.

I like the bug.

You like round.

I like long.

He likes short.

I like tall.

You like small.

I like one.

She likes more.

I like the flower.

We like the flowers.

the	round	short
bug	flower	tall
one	flowers	small
he	long	she

Words in this book

I	it	like
we	likes	you
more	they	dad
	mum	

Do you know the focus Core words: 'I' and 'like'? Read the words along each line.

like	I	like	I	I	like	I
I	like	I	like	I	like	like
I	like	like	I	like	I	like
like	I	I	like	like	I	like
I	like	like	I	I	like	I
like	like	I	like	I	like	like
I	like	I	like	like	I	like

Do you know the focus and secondary Core words in this book (refer to Core word table)? Find them along each line, point to them and say them. Read the other words too once you have pointed to the Core words.

I	the	round	I	we	like	long
you	I	like	flower	I	short	like
I	one	like	they	like	the	small
like	like	I	it	I	he	tall
dad	like	bug	I	likes	like	I
flowers	I	like	like	mum	bug	one
I	like	more	short	like	she	I

How many times did you read the word 'I'? How many times did you read the word 'like'?

Make new words with 'the__', e.g., 'there'. Write sentences using these words.

We hope you had fun reading!

VeeZee Publications

Wait, there's more!

Visit our website for information about our range of readers & supporting products.

veezeepublications.com

www.ingramcontent.com/pod-product-compliance
Lightning Source LLC
Chambersburg PA
CBHW050852010526

44107CB00047BA/1585